DRAFT

OF THE

JAPANESE CRIMINAL CODE

Translated from the Original Japanese Text
by J. E. de Becker (Kobayashi Beika)

Elibron Classics
www.elibron.com

Elibron Classics series.

ISBN 1-4021-7439-X (paperback)
ISBN 1-4212-8514-2 (hardcover)

This Elibron Classics Replica Edition is an unabridged facsimile of the edition published in 1899 by 'Eastern World', Yokohama.

This Code has not yet come before the Diet, and a few amendments are likely to be made before the next Diet is convoked. The foreign public has now the opportunity, therefore, and ample time, to acquaint themselves with the provisions of the new Criminal Code.

If amendments are made a supplement containing them will be furnished free of charge to purchasers of the book as soon as the Code has become law.

DRAFT

OF THE

JAPANESE CRIMINAL CODE.

(刑　法　草　案)

Translated from the Original Japanese Text

BY

J. E. de BECKER.

(*Kobayashi Beika.*)

Author of "KELLY & WALSH'S HANDBOOK OF THE JAPANESE LANGUAGE," "JAPANESE SELF-TAUGHT," and other works. Also translator of the 'Japanese Code of Criminal Procedure."

Printed at the "EASTERN WORLD" Office.

YOKOHAMA,

1899.

CONTENTS.

BOOK I.

GENERAL PROVISIONS.

BOOK II.

DIVISIONS OF CRIME.

BOOK I.

GENERAL PROVISIONS.

CHAPTER I.

OF THE APPLICATION OF THE PENAL CODE IN GENERAL.

ARTICLE 1.

Offences punishable by virtue of the law are felonies and delicts (misdemeanors).

ARTICLE 2.

If subsequent to the committal of an offence the punishment should be altered by (a new) law, the milder penalty (of the two laws) shall be applicable in cases where final judgment has not yet been rendered.

The rules of the new law shall be observed in respect to prescription and the execution of penalties.

ARTICLE 3.

The law is applicable to all offences committed within the borders of the Empire irrespective of whether the perpetrator be a native or an alien.

The law is also applicable to offences committed on board Japanese ships on the high seas, and to offences recognized as acts of piracy by International Law.

ARTICLE 4.

The law is applicable to offences committed by Japanese subjects in foreign countries where the Japanese possess extraterritorial rights.

Laws enforceable within the Empire exclusively form an exception to this article.

ARTICLE 5.

The law is also applicable to both Japanese subjects and aliens who, while resident in foreign countries, commit felonious acts against the Empire or its people.

ARTICLE 6.

The law is also applicable to the crimes of incendiarism, causing inundations, rape, and other crimes against life, the person, liberty, and property, committed by Japanese subjects in foreign countries.

It is likewise applicable to crimes committed by Japanese Government and public officials in foreign countries in connection with their official duties.

ARTICLE 7.

Even though the case may have been adjudicated upon in a foreign country and a final judgment rendered in respect to same, this shall be no bar to the institution of proceedings and the infliction of punishment (in Japan). If, however, the offender has already undergone the punishment to which he was sentenced in a foreign country, or any portion thereof, the Court may remit the execution of the penalty either in whole or in part.

ARTICLE 8.

Except in such cases where special rules exist the general provisions of this Penal Code are also applicable to the penalties determined by other laws.

CHAPTER II.

OF PENALTIES.

SECTION I.

PENALTIES.

ARTICLE 9.

The penalties for felonies are: —

Death.

Penal Servitude.

Imprisonment.
Deprivation of Civic rights.
Police surveillance.
Fine.

The penalties for misdemeanors are :—

Detention.
Police fine.

The accessory penalty for both felonies and misdemeanors is confiscation.

ARTICLE 10.

The penalty of death shall be executed by hanging in the interior of a prison.

ARTICLE 11.

No capital execution can be performed without an order from the Minister of Justice.

If a woman sentenced to death is *enceinte* the execution shall not be carried out, except in virtue of a special order issued subsequent to her delivery.

ARTICLE 12.

The execution of a capital penalty shall not be carried out on a national fête day or holiday.

ARTICLE 13.

Penal servitude is either perpetual or limited; limited penal servitude shall extend over a period of not less than one day and not exceeding fifteen years.

Persons condemned to penal servitude shall be detained in a convict establishment and subjected to forced labor determined by the regulations; a sentence of penal servitude for a period of less than six months may be carried out in a house of detention.

ARTICLE 14.

Imprisonment is either perpetual or limited; limited imprisonment shall extend over a period of not less than one day and not exceeding fifteen years.

Persons condemmed to imprisonment shall be detained in a prison, but shall not be subjected to obligatory labor except at their own request.

Imprisonment for a period of less than six months may be carried out in a house of detention.

ARTICLE 15.

The deprivation of Civic rights entails on the condemned :—

1. Loss of the rights of election and being elected.
2. Loss of Government and public official position, and consequent incapacity of performing their official functions connected therewith.
3. Incapacity of possessing decorations, pensions, or diplomas of rank.
4. Prohibition of wearing foreign decorations.
5. Incapacity of being enrolled on the registers of the army and navy.
6. Incapacity of becoming a guardian, supervisor of a guardian, advisor of a minor, or a member of the family council.

ARTICLE 16.

Deprivation of Civic rights is either perpetual or limited. Deprivation of Civic rights for a limited term extends over a period of not less than three and not exceeding fifteen years.

A sentence of deprivation of civic rights pronounceable simultaneously with a sentence of death, perpetual penal servitude, or perpetual imprisonment, is perpetual as a natural consequence.

A sentence of deprivation of civic rights pronounceable simultaneously with a sentence of limited penal servitude or limited imprisonment for upwards of ten years is either perpetual or limited, but if such penal servitude or imprisonment be limited to a period of under ten years the sentence of deprivation of civic rights pronounceable shall be less than ten years.

Persons who have been sentenced to deprivation of civic rights simultaneously with a sentence of limited penal servitude or limited imprisonment shall, as a natural consequence, be deprived of their civic rights until the expiration of the term of penal servitude or imprisonment, or until such time as the enforcement of the punishment be remitted.

ARTICLE 17.

Police surveillance entails on the condemned:—

1. The police authorities of the place where the crime was committed, or those of the place where the injured party resides, may forbid the person under surveillance entering either the whole or any part of the district under their jurisdiction.
2. Whenever the police deem it necessary so to do they may make a domiciliary search of the residence of the person under surveillance at any time and seize (suspicious or incriminating) objects.

ARTICLE 18.

The term of police surveillance shall not be less than one year nor exceed five years.

ARTICLE 19.

Persons who have been sentenced to death, perpetual penal servitude, or perpetual imprisonment, and have had the execution of the penalty remitted by pardon or prescription, or had the penalty reduced to a limited period of penal servitude or imprisonment, are to be regarded, as a matter of course, as sentenced to police surveillance for five years.

Persons who have been sentenced to penal servitude or imprisonment together with police surveillance and liberated on ticket-of-leave, are to be regarded, as a matter of course, as under police surveillance during the ticket-of-leave period.

ARTICLE 20.

Fines shall be from one *yen* upwards.

ARTICLE 21.

Persons who are unable to pay their fines in full shall be detained in prison for a period of not less than one day nor exceeding two years, and they may be subjected to forced labor.

The Court shall, simultaneously with pronouncing a sentence inflicting a fine, determine and state the (alternative) term of imprisonment in the event of non-payment in full.

When persons who have been sentenced to a fine have paid a moiety of the same they shall be imprisoned for the term specified in the judgment in lieu of fine, less such number of days as may correspond to the amount of money already paid, calculated in the same proportion as may exist between the entire fine and the full period of (alternative) imprisonment.

If during imprisonment the fine be paid the payment shall be calculated for the remaining number of days in the same proportion as specified in the foregoing paragraph.

ARTICLE 22.

Detention shall extend over a period of not less than one day and not exceeding one month, and the detained person shall be confined in a house of detention. Should the person detained make a request to that effect he may be subjected to labor in accordance with the regulations.

ARTICLE 23.

Police fines shall be from ten *sen* upwards but shall not exceed thirty *yen*.

ARTICLE 24.

When a person is unable to pay the whole of a police fine he shall be confined in a house of detention during a period of not less than one day nor more than one month, and he may be subjected to forced labour.

The Court when pronouncing a sentence inflicting a police fine shall at the same time render a decree fixing the term of detention in lieu of such fine should payment not be made in full.

The provisions of paragraphs 3 and 4 of Article 21 are also applicable to police fines.

ARTICLE 25.

The following articles may be confiscated, but only if they are the property of the offender or ownerless :—

1. Objects which have constituted the crime.
2. Objects which have been used in committing a crime.
3. Objects acquired by means of a crime.

ARTICLE 26.

In connection with the punishment of a misdemeanor confiscation cannot be enforced unless in virtue of a special provision of the law.

SECTION II.

OF THE CALCULATION OF THE DURATION OF PENALTIES.

ARTICLE 27.

The duration of penalties is calculated at the rate of 24 hours to a day and 30 days to a month, while the year is reckoned according to the almanac.

The day on which the penalty has begun to be executed is reckoned as an entire day.

Liberation is effected on the morning of the day following the last day of the duration of a penalty.

Article 28.

The duration of penalties is reckoned from the day following the day on which final judgment has been rendered.

The days during which the accused has not been imprisoned even after final judgment has been rendered are not reckoned for him in the duration of the penalties of penal servitude, imprisonment, and detention.

The term of deprivation of civic rights and/or police surveillance, to which the accused has been sentenced simultaneously with a sentence of limited penal servitude or imprisonment, is calculated from the day following the day on which the period of such imprisonment expires, or its execution be remitted.

The period of police surveillance over persons who have had the penalties of death, perpetual penal servitude, or perpetual imprisonment remitted is calculated from the day following the day on which such remission was granted.

With regard to the period of police surveillance over persons who have had their sentences reduced from death, perpetual penal servitude, or perpetual imprisonment to limited penal servitude, or limited imprisonment, the provisions of the preceding paragraph are applicable.

Article 29.

The days during which the accused has been held in custody pending trial shall be included in the calculation of the duration of penalty according to the following distinctions.

The number of days during which the accused has been held in custody pending trial shall not be taken into consideration when such period of time is less than the equivalent of one day, or of one *yen*, of the principal penalty.

1. Six days of custody to each day of penal servitude.

2. Three days of custody to each day of imprisonment or detention.
3. Two days of custody to each *yen* of fine or police fine, but even if the amount is less than a *yen* the same rule applies.

SECTION III.

On the (Conditional) Suspension and Remission of Penalties.

Article 30.

With regard to a person who has been sentenced to less than six months penal servitude or imprisonment for a first offence, he may, according to the circumstances of the case, acquire the benefit of (conditional) suspension of the sentence during the period of prescription from the day on which judgment has been rendered.

Article 31.

With regard to a person who has been sentenced to be fined for a first offence, and who should be detained owing to his inability to pay the fine in full, he may acquire the benefit of (conditional) suspension of the execution of the sentence during the period of prescription in accordance with the provisions of the preceding article irrespective of the number of days involved, but this provision does not apply to persons who should undergo the penalties of penal servitude or imprisonment.

Article 32.

Even persons who have been sentenced to penal servitude or imprisonment for terms of more than six months may acquire (conditional) suspension of the execution of their sentences in accordance with the provisions of Article 30 if the penalty has been reduced in consideration of their voluntary denunciation and if the case is of such a nature that no direct injury has been done to the life, person, or liberty of third parties or it is a case where the offence against property has been fully compensated.

ARTICLE 33.

With regard to the (conditional) suspension of the execution of a sentence, the Court shall render a decision in accordance with the statement of the Public Procurator prior to the execution of the penalty.

In this case execution of the penalty shall be suspended pending the decision of the Court.

ARTICLE 34.

The provisions of Articles 30 to 32 are not applicable to persons who have been sentenced to deprivation of civic rights or to police surveillance.

ARTICLE 35.

Persons who have committed no further grave offences (other than finable ones) during the term of the (conditional) suspension of their sentences shall have such (conditionally) suspended penalties remitted (in full).

ARTICLE 36.

In the case of persons who have committed a further grave offence, other than a finable one, during the term of conditional suspension of their sentences, they shall, as a natural consequence, suffer the previous penalty and also the subsequently imposed penalty.

ARTICLE 37.

In the case of persons who have been sentenced to penal servitude or imprisonment and about whom it is considered that there is no fear of their again committing a felony, a ticket-of-leave may be granted to them by an administrative measure after the lapse of one third of the whole term of a limited penalty, or of fifteen years of a perpetual penalty.

ARTICLE 38.

Persons who have committed no further grave offences (other than finable ones) during the term of their liberation on a ticket of leave shall have the execution of the penalties of penal servitude or imprisonment remitted in full, but in the event of their committing a felony, other than a finable one, the period of their (conditional) release on ticket of leave shall not be reckoned for them in calculating the term of their penalties.

ARTICLE 39.

Persons who have been sentenced to detention, may at any time, have such sentence remitted by an administrative measure according to the circumstances of the case. The same rule applies to the case of persons under detention in consequence of their inability to pay fines or police fines in full and also to the case of persons sentenced to penitentiary discipline.

SECTION IV.

PRESCRIPTION.

ARTICLE 40.

Prescription is acquired by condemned persons who have evaded (escaped?) the execution of their penalties during the terms fixed by law.

ARTICLE 41.

The terms of prescription are as follows :—

1. 30 years for a capital penalty :
2. 20 years for perpetual penal servitude or perpetual imprisonment :

3. 15 years for limited penal servitude or limited imprisonment of upwards of 10 years: 10 years for limited penal servitude or limited imprisonment of upwards of 3 years: 5 years for limited penal servitude or limited imprisonment of less than 3 years:
4. 3 years for fines:
5. 1 year for detention, police fines, or confiscation.

Article 42.

Prescription cannot be acquired in respect to deprivation of civic rights or police surveillance.

Article 43.

The duration of prescription shall be calculated from the day of escape from detention with a view to avoiding execution of the penalty; in case of the condemned not having been under arrest the calculation shall be made as from the day on which final judgment has been rendered.

Calculation *re* fines, police fines, and confiscations shall be made as from the day on which final judgment has been rendered.

Article 44.

Prescription is interrupted by the arrest of of the condemned for the purpose of enforcing the execution of the penalty, or by the issue of an order by the Minister of Justice, *re* his arrest.

SECTION V.

Of Amnesty, Pardon, Mitigation, and Rehabilitation.

Article 45.

Amnesty annuls the effect of any judgment that has been rendered, but in case of a fine or police fine already paid, or in case of objects already confiscated, no claim is admissable for a return of such monies or objects.

ARTICLE 46.

Amnesty remits the execution of the penalty and mitigation reduces it.

ARTICLE 47.

Rehabilitation restores civic rights for the future and implies the placing of the rehabilitated person beyond police surveillance as a natural consequence.

CHAPTER III.

EXEMPTION FROM PENALTIES AND LEGAL EXCUSES.

ARTICLE 48.

Acts performed in accordance with the law, or in the discharge of one's legal and proper (official ?) duties, are not punishable.

ARTICLE 49.

Acts performed under the stress of necessity for the protection of one's own or another's rights in cases of imminent peril, arising from a sudden and unlawful attack, are not punishable, but this rule does not hold good when the accused has invited the attack by his own improper or unlawful conduct.

If the act has exceeded the limits of necessity the penalty may be lowered according to the circumstances of the case.

ARTICLE 50.

The punishment of acts performed under the stress of acute necessity in order to save from imminent danger the life, person, liberty, or property of one's self or another, shall, according to the circumstances of the case, either be reduced or remitted in full.

This rule is not applicable to persons who have special duties (to discharge ?) appertaining to their official functions.

ARTICLE 51.

There is exemption from penalty when the accused has not had the intention of committing an infraction, save in cases in which the law punishes negligence.

Ignorance of the law or regulations cannot be invoked to establish absence of design.

ARTICLE 52.

The acts of persons who are *non compos mentis,* or suffering from alienation of mind, are not punishable, but according to the circumstances of the case they may be ordered to be placed under supervisory restraint.

ARTICLE 53.

The acts of infants under the age of ten years are not punishable, but when the act constitutes a felony and the age of the infant exceeds eight years, he may, according to the circumstances of the case, be ordered to be placed under reformatory discipline until he attains his fifteenth year but no longer.

ARTICLE 54.

The acts of infants over ten and under 15 years of age are not punishable when they are unable to discriminate between right and wrong, but when the act constitutes a felony they may, according to the circumstances of the case, he ordered to be placed under reformatory discipline until they attain their twentieth year but no longer.

If they have acted with discernment when committing an infraction the penalty shall be lowered.

ARTICLE 55.

Penalties may be lowered in the case of acts committed by persons over fifteen and under twenty years of age.

Article 56.

Penalties for acts of deaf mutes shall either be lowered or remitted in full, but in the event of punishment not being inflicted they may, according to the circumstances of the case, be ordered to be placed under reformatory discipline for a term not exceeding five years.

Article 57.

The penalty shall be lowered when the offender has denounced himself to the authorities prior to their obtaining official cognizance of the act.

In cases where the complaint of the injured party should be awaited before official action is taken, if the offender denounces himself to the injured party, the benefit to such offender is the same as if he denounced himself to the authorities.

CHAPTER IV.

Of Infractions not Consummated.

Article 58.

When the execution of an offence has been actually commenced, but has not been consummated by reason of fortuitous circumstances, the penalty shall be lowered.

When infractions not consummated are punished each case shall be determined in accordance with this article.

Article 59.

In the case of a person having commenced the execution of an offence and voluntarily desisted from the attempt he shall be punished according to the actual results of such overt act.

CHAPTER V.

Of the Concurrence of Several Offences.

Article 60.

Several infractions in respect to which final judgment has not yet been rendered, shall be deemed concurrent offences.

Should final judgment have been rendered with regard to one infraction, then only that particular infraction, and the offence (s) committed prior to such final judgment having been rendered shall be considered as concurrent offences.

Article 61.

If among concurrent offences one is punishable by death, the penalties for the other offences (with the exception of deprivation of civic rights and confiscation) shall not be imposed.

If one of the offences is punishable by unlimited penal servitude or unlimited imprisonment, in this case also the penalties for the other offences (with the exception of deprivation of civic rights, fine, police fine, and confiscation) shall not be imposed.

Article 62.

When there are upwards of two concurrent offences punishable by limited penal servitude or imprisonment, the maximum term shall be that of the penalty for the most serious of the offences increased by one half. The maximum term shall not exceed the total accumulative term of all the various and several inflictable penalties added together.

Although among the penalties for grave offences there are no short terms, yet when a short term is an applicable penalty for some other offence the penalty shall not be lighter than such short term. In the event of there being two or more short terms, the penalty shall not be reduced below the heaviest among them.

Of penal servitude and imprisonment, the former is the more severe penalty, but when the term of imprisonment exceeds that of the duration of penal servitude the most severe penalty is that of imprisonment. The duration of imprisonment is compared with that of penal servitude in the ratio of two to one.

Article 63.

Fines and other penalties shall be concurrently imposed, except in the case provided for in the first paragraph of Article 61.

When more than two fines are imposed the cumulative amount of such fines shall be less than the total of all the fines imposable for each offence.

Article 64.

Deprivation of Civic rights, Police surveillance, and other penalties, shall be imposed concurrently. Should there be more than two concurrent instances of Deprivation of Civic rights and Police surveillance the longest of the terms shall be imposed.

Article 65.

Confiscation shall be imposed concurrently.

Article 66.

When among concurrent crimes one (or more) has been adjudicated upon, and the other not yet tried, the offence not yet adjudicated upon shall be separately tried and decided, and the punishments determined both for the former as well as the latter shall be concurrently enforced.

When in accordance with the foregoing paragraph the death penalty should be executed, other penalties (with the exception of deprivation of civic rights and confiscation) shall not be enforced. When the offence is punishable by unlimited penal servitude or imprisonment, other penalties (with the exception of deprivation of civic rights, fine, police fine, and confiscation) shall not be enforced. With regard to the enforcement of the penalties of limited penal servitude and imprisonment, the maximum term imposable in respect to the most serious crimes may not be augmented by more than half such maximum term. The provisions of paragraph 3, Article 62 are also applicable to the execution of limited penal servitude and imprisonment.

As regards deprivation of civic rights and police surveillance the longest term shall be enforced.

Article 67.

When two or more final judgments have been rendered in respect to concurrent offences such judgments shall be enforced in accordance with the provisions of the preceding article.

Article 68.

When a person has been dealt with in respect to concurrent offences and been pardoned with regard to one (or more) of them by reason of an amnesty, the Court shall, according to the conditions of the letter of pardon, make a special order determining the penalty for the offence (or offences) not included in such amnesty.

Article 69.

Penalties for misdemeanors shall be imposed concurrently, except in such cases as are provided for in Article 61.

Article 70.

With regard to criminal acts, either isolated or correlative, describable by various names, these shall be dealt with and punished by the imposition of the most severe penalty. The provisions of Article 62, paragraph 3, and Article 65 are also applicable in the cases contemplated by this article.

CHAPTER VI.

Of the Repetition of Offences.

Article 71.

When a person is sentenced to penal servitude for a certain offence, and within ten years from the day on which the execution of the penalty ceased, or was remitted, he again commits another offence of a similar nature, such offence shall be considered as a "repeated offence."

The same also applies to a person who has had a sentence of death remitted.

Article 72.

When a person has previously been sentenced with regard to concurrent offences, and is guilty of an infraction punishable by an augmented penalty by reason of its being a repetition of some offence or offences comprised among such concurrent offences, the penalty shall be augmented in the case of "repeated offences" even although such repeated offences themselves may not constitute infractions of the most serious nature.

Article 73.

Offences which should be punished with augmented severity owing to their being "repeated offences," shall each be determined under this article.

ARTICLE 74.

Punishments for "repeated offences," with the exception of deprivation of Civic rights and police surveillance, shall be twice as severe as the ordinary penalties provided by law for the respective offences.

ARTICLE 75.

When, after final judgment has been given, it is discovered that the person is one who has committed a "repeated offence" the penalty to be augmented shall be determined in accordance with the provisions of the preceding articles by order of the Court.

ARTICLE 76.

The provisions *re* "repeated offences" are likewise applicable even in the case of persons who have committed infractions three times or more.

CHAPTER VII.

OF CO-OPERATION OF SEVERAL PERSONS IN THE SAME OFFENCE.

ARTICLE 77.

When two or more persons have united in the commission of an offence they shall be regarded as principals.

ARTICLE 78.

Persons who have instigated others in the commission of an offence shall be regarded as principals.

ARTICLE 79.

Persons who have assisted principal offenders shal be egarded as accomplices.

ARTICLE 80.

Instigators who have instigated other instigators shall be regarded as principals, and persons who have assisted instigators, or instigated accomplices, shall be regarded as accomplices.

ARTICLE 81.

As regards the punishment of accomplices the penalties imposable shall be compared with those on principals, and in case of the reduction of penalties the same proportion shall be observed.

ARTICLE 82.

In the case of a misdemeanor, neither instigators nor accomplices are punishable except by virtue of a special provision of the law.

ARTICLE 83.

When persons have been participators in an act which constitutes a crime by reason of the social status of the principal offender, they shall be regarded as joint offenders, even although their relative social positions may not be identical with his.

When the severity of a penalty is specially determined according to the social status or rank of the offender, the ordinary penalty shall be inflicted on persons occupying a position lower than that of the principal.

CHAPTER VIII.

OF EXTENUATING CIRCUMSTANCES.

ARTICLE 84.

When extenuating circumstances exist in favour of an offender, the Court may consider the same and reduce the penalty accordingly.

ARTICLE 58.

Even in cases where the (text of the) law governs and determines the raising or lowering of penalties the Court may (go a step further and) take extenuating circumstances into consideration and reduce the penalty.

CHAPTER IX.

OF THE AGGRAVATION AND COMMUTATION OF PENALTIES.

ARTICLE 86.

Except in cases where the punishment is lightened on account of extenuating circumstances, when there exists one or more causes for mitigating penalties such penalties shall be lowered as follows:—

1. When the punishment of death is to be mitigated it shall be commuted either to perpetual penal servitude or imprisonment or for a period of not less than 7 years:
2. When the punishment of perpetual penal servitude or imprisonment is to be mitigated, it shall be commuted either to penal servitude or imprisonment for a period of not less than 5 years:
3. When either limited penal servitude, or limited imprisonment, or detention, is to be mitigated, it shall be commuted by not more than two thirds the maximum period, but in such cases where the minimum term is specially determined in various articles of the law commutation by one third of such minimum term shall be considered the minimum period:
4. Commutation of fine or police-fine shall not exceed two thirds of the maximum amount.

Article 87.

Except in cases where the punishment is lightened on account of extenuating circumstances, when penalties shall be mitigated and there are more than two (penalties), the particular penalty to be inflicted shall be first determined upon and it shall then be lowered.

Article 88.

When penalties should be mitigated in consideration of extenuating circumstances the following rules are to be followed:—

1. When the punishment of death is to be mitigated, perpetual penal servitude or imprisonment shall be imposed:
2. When the punishment of perpetual penal servitude or imprisonment is to be mitigated, limited penal servitude or imprisonment shall be imposed:
3. When the punishment of limited penal servitude or imprisonment, for which a minimum term is provided, is to be mitigated, a term of penal servitude or imprisonment less than the minimum period shall be imposed.

Article 89.

When there exist simultaneously causes in aggravation and extenuation of the penalty, these causes are considered in the following order:

1. Aggravation of penalty on account of the repetition of the offence:
2. Legal excuses:
3. Aggravation of penalty on account of concurrence of offences:
4. Extenuating circumstances.

Article 90.

Limited penal servitude $\frac{\text{and}}{\text{or}}$ imprisonment cannot be augmented so as to exceed a period of thirty years.

Deprivation of civic rights and Police surveillance shall neither be augmented nor mitigated.

BOOK II.

CHAPTER I.

OF OFFENCES AGAINST THE PERSON OF THE EMPEROR, AND MEMBERS OF THE IMPERIAL FAMILY.

ARTICLE 91.

Execution or contrivance of acts of violence against the person of the Emperor, the Empress, the Emperor's Grandmother, the Empress Dowager, the Crown Prince, or the heir presumptive, shall be punished with death.

ARTICLE 92.

Acts of an insulting and disrespectful nature committed against the Emperor, the Empress, the Emperor's Grandmother, the Empress Dowager, the Crown Prince, or the heir presumptive, shall be punished with penal servitude for a period not exceeding five years.

The same law applies in the case of insulting and disrespecful acts committed against the Imperial Ancestors, or the Emperor of the previous reign.

ARTICLE 93.

Execution of acts of violence against the persons of the members of the Imperial family shall be punished with death: attempts to commit such acts shall be punished with perpetual penal servitude.

ARTICLE 94.

Acts of an insulting and disrespectful nature committed against members of the Imperial family shall be punished with penal servitude not exceeding four years.

The same law applies to cases where any insulting and disrespectful act has been committed against members of the Imperial family of the preceding generation.

ARTICLE 95.

Persons who have committed offences mentioned in this chapter, and are therefore punishable with limited penal servitude, shall also be placed under police surveillance.

CHAPTER II.

OF OFFENCES AGAINST THE INTERNAL SAFETY (GOVERNMENT) OF THE STATE.

ARTICLE 96.

Persons who have been guilty of committing seditious acts of violence with the object of seizing the territories of the state, or subverting the government and laws of the Empire, shall, according to the nature of their participation, be punished as follows:—

1. With death or perpetual imprisonment those who have been the ringleaders:
2. With perpetual imprisonment, or imprisonment for not less than five years, those who have participated in the conspiracy or held a command in the insurrectionary body. Persons who have been engaged in the sedition in various other official capacities shall be punished with imprisonment for a period not exceeding ten years:
3. With imprisonment for a period not exceeding five years, persons who have been mere participators in the outbreak in the capacity of ordinary followers.

In the case of offences mentioned in this article infractions not consummated are also punishable.

Article 97.

Persons who have conspired to raise an insurrection and/or made preparations to commit violent and seditious acts, shall be punished with imprisonment for a period not exceeding ten years.

Article 98.

Persons who have aided and abetted the insurrection by furnishing arms and munitions of war, monies and provisions, and otherwise assisted in the committal of acts of violence, or in promoting preparations and/or intrigues relative to the same, shall be punished with imprisonment for a period not exceeding seven years.

Article 99.

Persons who have committed offences mentioned in this chapter, and who are therefore punishable with death, perpetual servitude, perpetual imprisonment, or imprisonment exceeding one year, shall also be sentenced to deprivation of civil rights.

Article 100.

Persons who, although having participated in acts preliminary to an insurrectionary movement, have voluntarily denounced themselves to the authorities before the beginning of its execution shall be exempted from punishment.

CHAPTER III.

Of offences against the external safety of the State.

Article 101.

Persons who have conspired with any foreign power to commence hostilities against the Empire, or who have joined alien enemies in fighting against the Empire, shall be punished with death.

Article 102.

Persons who have delivered to the enemy any castle, fortress, camp, body of troops, ports, harbours, vessels of war $\frac{\text{and}}{\text{or}}$ other ships, or grounds and buildings devoted to military purposes, shall be punished with death.

Persons who have delivered to the enemy arms $\frac{\text{and}}{\text{or}}$ munitions of war, or otherwise supplied objects directly employed in military operations, shall be punished with death or perpetual penal servitude.

Article 103.

Persons who have delivered to the enemy privately owned arms, munitions of war, ships, $\frac{\text{and}}{\text{or}}$ other objects directly employed in military operations, shall be punished with perpetual penal servitude, or penal servitude for a period of not less than five years.

Article 104.

Persons who, for the purpose of aiding the enemy, have damaged or rendered unfit for use, any castle, fortress, camp, port, harbour, vessels of war $\frac{\text{and}}{\text{or}}$ other ships, arms, munitions of war, steam cars, electric cars, railroads, telegraph lines, or grounds and buildings devoted to military purposes, belonging to or held and used by the Japanese Empire, shall be punished with death or perpetual penal servitude.

Article 105.

Persons who have acted as spies for the enemy, or assisted the enemy's spies, shall be punished with death, perpetual penal servitude, or penal servitude for a period of not less than seven years.

The same law is applicable to persons who have divulged military or political secrets to the enemy.

Even when not in time of war, persons who have divulged to foreign countries the secrets mentioned in the foregoing paragraph shall be punished with limited penal servitude.

Article 106.

Persons who have, by the use of methods other than those mentioned in the several foregoing articles, aided the enemy in military matters $\frac{\text{and}}{\text{or}}$ injured the military interests of the Empire, shall be punished with limited penal servitude.

Article 107.

The offences mentioned in Articles 101 to 106 are punishable even when not consummated.

Article 108.

Persons who have made preparations and intrigued with the intention of committing the offences mentioned in Articles 101 to 106, shall be punished with penal servitude for a period not exceeding ten years.

Article 109.

Persons who have been guilty of the offences mentioned in this chapter and who are punishable with death or penal servitude, shall be sentenced to deprivation of civic rights, and persons punishable with limited penal servitude shall be sentenced to deprivation of civic rights and also to police surveillance.

ARTICLE 110.

The provisions of this chapter are only applicable to aliens when offences are committed by persons actually residing within the Japanese Empire.

ARTICLE 111.

The provisions of this chapter are also applicable to acts committed against an ally of the Empire in time of war.

CHAPTER IV.

OF OFFENCES AGAINST NATIONAL INTERCOURSE.

ARTICLE 112.

Persons who have committed acts of violence (*bō-kō*) against the Sovereign or President of a Treaty Power sojourning in the Empire, shall be punished with penal servitude for a period of not less than one year and not exceeding ten years.

In such cases where the acts committed are of the nature of insults (*bu-joku*) they are punishable with penal servitude for a period not exceeding three years, but the prosecution shall only take place on the complaint of the foreign government concerned.

ARTICLE 113.

Persons who have committed acts of an insulting nature against an ambassador of a Treaty Power accredited to the Japanese Empire, shall be punished with penal servitude for a period not exceeding one year, but the prosecution shall only take place on the complaint of the injured party.

Article 114.

Persons who have damaged, soiled, or removed the national flag or other national emblem of any Treaty Power with the object of insulting such Treaty Power, shall be punished either with penal servitude for a period not exceeding two years or a fine not exceeding two hundred *yen*: the prosecution, however, shall only take place on the complaint of the foreign government concerned.

Article 115.

Persons who have made preparations and intrigued with the object of waging private war against a Treaty Power, shall be punished with imprisonment for a period not exceeding five years, but in case of their voluntarily denouncing themselves to the authorities the penalty will be remitted.

Article 116.

Persons who have violated a decree of neutrality when foreign nations are at war shall be punished with imprisonment for a period not exceeding one year or a fine of not exceeding five hundred *yen*. In the case of Japanese subjects, those who have violated the rules of neutrality while resident in foreign countries are likewise punishable under the provisions of this article.

CHAPTER V.

Of offences against Public Rights.

SECTION I.

Of Interference with the Exercise of Public Functions.

Article 117.

Persons who have committed acts of (personal) violence against, or intimidated, government officials, public officials, or members of any public representative body with the intention of obstructing them in the performance of their duties or causing them to take official action in any matter, shall be punished with penal servitude for a period not exceeding four years.

The provisions of this article are also applicable to persons who have committed acts of (personal) violence against, or intimidated, government offices, public offices or any public representative body.

Article 118.

Persons who have committed acts of (personal) violence against, or intimidated, government officials, public officials, or members of any public representative body, with the intention of causing them to resign their positions, shall be punished with penal servitude for a period not exceeding three years.

Article 119.

Persons who have insulted government officials, private officials, or members of any public representative body in the performance of their duties and in their presence, or insulted them, in their official capacity although not in their actual presence, by means of writings, pictures, and images publicly exhibited, or by public theatrical representations, songs, or public discourses, shall be punished with penal servitude for a period not exceeding one year or with the imposition of a fine not exceeding one hundred *yen*.

Persons who have insulted government offices, public offices, or any public representative body by means of writings, pictures, or images publicly exhibited, or by public theatrical representations, songs, or public discourses, shall be punished in like manner.

Article 120.

Persons who have damaged, or soiled, seals or marks, indicative of attachment, affixed by government or public officials, thereby rendering the said seals or marks null and void, shall be punished with penal servitude for a period not exceeding one year, or with the imposition of a fine not exceeding one hundred *yen*.

SECTION II.

Of offences relative to elections.

Article 121.

Persons who have, during an election of members of a public representative body, or of government officials, either committed acts of violence, used threats of force, or been guilty of fraudulent devices or corrupt practices in order to induce any voter to vote either on his own behalf, or on behalf of any other person, or to prevent the exercise of the electoral franchise, shall be punished with penal servitude for a period not exceeding three years, or with the imposition of a fine not exceeding two hundred *yen*.

Article 122.

Persons who have, with the intentions mentioned in the foregoing article, given, or agreed to give, any money, goods, or other valuable consideration, or pecuniary advantage, shall be punished with penal servitude for a period not exceeding two years, or with the imposition of a fine not exceeding three hundred *yen*.

Persons who have received, or agreed to receive, any of the above-mentioned benefits, are punishable with a fine not exceeding fifty *yen*.

Article 123.

Persons who have committed offences mentioned in this Section, and are punishable with upwards of one year's penal servitude, shall also be sentenced to deprivation of civic rights.

SECTION III.

of the Escape of Prisoners.

Article 124.

Every prisoner, whether convicted or unconvicted, who shall have escaped, shall be punished with penal servitude for a period not exceeding one year.

If the escape has been effected by means of damaging or breaking the prison or its furniture and fittings, by acts of violence, or intimidation by menace of injury, or if upwards of two prisoners secretly working in concert have escaped, the offender or offenders shall be punished with penal servitude for a period not exceeding three years.

Article 125.

Every individual who, by the aid of violence or intimidation, shall have removed a prisoner from custody, or shall have assisted his escape, shall be punished with penal servitude for a period of not less than one year and not exceeding ten years.

Article 126.

Persons who shall have supplied to a prisoner, with the object of enabling him to escape, lethal weapons or tools, or in any other way assisted the escape of a prisoner, shall be punished with penal servitude for a period of not exceeding five years.

ARTICLE 127.

Gaolers and guards who have (wittingly) allowed prisoners to escape, shall be punished with penal servitude for a period not exceeding ten years.

ARTICLE 128.

The offences mentioned in this Section are punishable even when not consummated.

SECTION IV.

OF THE CONCEALMENT OF OFFENDERS AND THE SUPPRESSION AND DESTRUCTION OF PROOFS OF GUILT.

ARTICLE 129.

Persons who have harbored or concealed, or have assisted the flight of an escaped prisoner who has committed an act rendering him liable to be criminally punished as for a grave offence (except when such punishment consists merely of a fine), shall be punished with penal servitude for a period not exceeding two years or a fine of not exceeding one hundred *yen*.

ARTICLE 130.

Persons who have suppressed, destroyed, forged, or fraudulently altered (documentary) evidence relating to a case in which another party is a defendant in a criminal trial, shall be punished with penal servitude for a period not exceeding one year or a fine of not exceeding one hundred *yen*.

ARTICLE 131.

When the offences mentioned in this Section are committed by .blood relations of a criminal defendant, for his benefit or in his interest, they will not be punished.

CHAPTER VI.

OF OFFENCES AGAINST THE PUBLIC PEACE.

SECTION I.

UNLAWFUL ASSEMBLY.

ARTICLE 132.

No matter what their object may be, persons who have assembled together in large numbers, and, in order to execute their common purpose, have acted in a violent and turbulent manner or been guilty of intimidation by menace of injury, shall be dealt with as follows :—

1. Ringleaders shall be punished with penal servitude for a period not exceeding ten years :
2. Persons who have led or directed others and forwarded the aforesaid acts shall be punished with penal servitude for a period not exceeding seven years :
3. Those who have simply participated in these acts shall be punished with a fine of not exceeding fifty *yen*.

ARTICLE 133.

Persons who have assembled together in large numbers, with the intention of executing their common purpose by means of violence and intimidation, and have refused to disperse although required by a government or public officer so to do, shall be punished, if ringleaders, with penal servitude for a period not exceeding three years, and others with a fine of not exceeding fifty *yen*.

ARTICLE 134.

Persons who have committed any of the offences mentioned in this Section, and are consequently punishable with penal servitude for upwards of one year, may also be sentenced to deprivation of civic rights.

SECTION II.

Of the Illegal Manufacture and Possession of Arms and Munitions of War.

Article 135.

Persons who have manufactured, imported, or sold fire-arms $^{\text{and}}_{\text{or}}$ ammunition without being duly licensed to do so, shall be punished with penal servitude for a period not exceeding one year, or a fine of not exceeding five hundred *yen*.

Attempts to commit the offences mentioned in this article shall be punishable even if the offences be not actually consummated.

Article 136.

Persons guilty of secretly holding or possessing any of the objects mentioned in the foregoing article shall be punished with a fine of not exceeding one hundred *yen*.

SECTION III.

Of Arson and accidental Conflagrations.

Article 137.

Whosoever shall have (wilfully) set fire to buildings actually inhabited and used as dwelling houses, or to buildings, steam-cars, electric cars, boats, or mines, actually containing persons, shall be punished with death, perpetual penal servitude, or penal servitude for a period of not less than seven years.

Article 138.

Whosoever shall have (wilfully) set fire to buildings not actually inhabited and in use as dwelling-houses, or to buildings, steam-cars, electric cars, boats, or mines, not actually containing persons, shall be punished with penal servitude for life, or for a period of not less than five years.

Persons who have (wilfully) set fire to any of the objects mentioned in the foregoing paragraph, being their own property, shall be punished with penal servitude for a period not exceeding five years.

Article 139.

Persons who have (wilfully) set fire to any wood, coppice, or plantation of bamboo or other trees, or to any crops of hay, grass, corn, or grain, standing or cut down and deposited in the fields, straw, hay, wood, bamboos, or any other objects happening to be stacked up in the open, shall be punished with penal servitude for a period not exceeding ten years.

Even although the various objects mentioned in the preceeding paragraph are the property of the incendiary himself, if by reason of the act of (wilfully) setting fire to them there has been a danger of a common (public) peril arising therefrom, the offender shall be punished with penal servitude for a period not exceeding two years or a fine of not exceeding one hundred *yen* : should the fire have spread to and burned the property of another person, then the punishment shall be penal servitude for a period not exceeding five years.

Article 140.

Attempts to commit any of the offenses mentioned in the foregoing three articles shall be punished even if the offences are not actually consummated.

Article 141.

When a person has (wilfully) set fire to any of the objects mentioned in articles 138 and 139, and such objects happen to be under attachment, hypothecated, borrowed, or insured, he shall be punished just as if he had set fire to and burned another person's property, even although they may actually be the property of the offender himself.

ARTICLE 142.

Persons who have (wilfully) hidden, damaged, or destroyed apparatus used in extinguishing fires, or by any other means obstructed the stamping out of a conflagration, shall be punished with penal servitude for a period not exceeding seven years.

ARTICLE 143.

Persons who have committed the offences mentioned in Articles 137 to 139, 141 and 142 and are punishable with death or perpetual penal servitude *may* be sentenced to deprivation of civic rights. Persons who are punishable with limited penal servitude for a period exceeding one year *may* be sentenced to deprivation of civic rights and placed under police surveillance.

ARTICLE 144.

Persons who have by fault or negligence accidentally burnt any of the objects mentioned in Articles 137 to 139 and 141 shall be punished with a fine of not exceeding fifty *yen*.

ARTICLE 145.

Persons who have wilfully caused an explosion of gunpowder, steam-boilers, or of explosive substances, and thereby damaged or destroyed any of the objects mentioned in Articles 137 tc 139 and 141, shall be punished as guilty of either arson or of causing an accidental fire.

SECTION IV.

Of Inundations.

Article 146.

Whosoever shall have (wilfully) caused an inundation and thus caused damage to buildings actually inhabited and used as dwelling houses, or to buildings, steam-cars, electric cars, or mines actually containing persons, shall be punished with death, perpetual penal servitude, or penal servitude for a period of not less than seven years.

Article 147.

Whosoever shall have (wilfully) caused an inundation, and thus damaged buildings not actually inhabited and in use as dwellinghouses, or to buildings, steam-cars, electric cars, or mines not actually containing persons, shall be punished with penal servitude for life or for a period of not less than five years.

Article 148.

Persons who have (wilfully) caused an inundation, and thereby occasioned damage to objects besides those mentioned in the two preceding articles, shall be punished with penal servitude for life or for a period not exceeding ten years.

Article 149.

When a person has (wilfully) caused inundation, and thereby occasioned damage to objects mentioned in articles 146 and 147, even although such objects are his own property if they are under attachment, hypothecated, borrowed or insured, he shall be punished just as if he had caused flooding of the property of another.

Article 150.

Persons who have (wilfully) concealed, broken or destroyed, any objects used to dam out water in time of flood, or by any other means obstructed the damming out of the waters, shall be punished with penal servitude for a period not exceeding seven years.

Article 151.

Persons who have committed the offences mentioned in Articles 146 to 150, and who are punishable with death or perpetual penal servitude, *may* be sentenced to deprivation of civic rights; Persons who are punishable with limited penal servitude for a period exceeding one year *may* be sentenced to deprivation of civic rights and placed under police surveillance.

Article 152.

Persons who have by fault or negligence acidentally caused flooding of any of the objects mentioned in Articles 146 to 149, shall be punished with a fine of not exceeding fifty *yen*.

Article 153.

Whosoever shall have (wilfully) destroyed sluices or broken embankments of a river or stream, or otherwise done anything to injure water-courses, water-ways, streams or channels, or done anything calculated to cause an inundation, shall be punished with penal servitude for a period not exceeding three years or a fine of not exceeding one hundred *yen*.

SECTION V.

Of the Destruction of and Damage to the Means of Communication.

Article 154.

Those who shall have (wilfully) destroyed or damaged a public road or water-way, or obstructed the traffic thereon, shall be punished with penal servitude for a period not exceeding three years or a fine of not exceeding two hundred *yen*.

Article 155.

If in the cases foreseen in the preceding article there has resulted a death or wounds, comparison shall be made with the offences of "Wounding and (grievous) bodily harm" and the offender shall be punished) according to the seriousness of the case.

Article 156.

They shall be punished with limited penal servitude for a period of not exceeding three years who have, by (wilfully) damaging the track or the signals of a railway, or, by any means whatsoever, exposed steam or electric cars to danger during transit over the lines.

The penalty imposed shall also be applicable to those who have exposed ships to danger by destroying or damaging lighthouses or buoys, or by any other means.

Article 157.

Persons who have (wilfully) upset or damaged steam and electric cars shall be punished with penal servitude for life or not less than five years.

The penalty for causing shipwreck or damage to a ship is the same.

ARTICLE 158.

The punishment of persons who have committed the offences mentioned in article 156 and thereby overturned or injured any steam or electric cars, or wrecked or destroyed vessels, shall be the same as that specified in the preceding article.

ARTICLE 159.

Persons who have committed the offences mentioned in the preceding two articles, and thereby caused loss of life, shall be punished either with death or perpetual penal servitude.

ARTICLE 160.

Even when the offences mentioned in Articles 154, 156, and 157 are not actually consummated, the attempt to commit them shall be punished.

ARTICLE 161.

When the acts mentioned in articles 156 and 157 have resulted from negligence the punishment shall be a fine of not exceeding three hundred *yen*.

When persons have committed the offences mentioned in the preceding paragraph in the course of their professional duties, they shall be punished with imprisonment for a period of not exceeding three years or by the imposition of a fine of not exceeding five hundred *yen*.

ARTICLE 162.

Persons who have (wilfully) damaged anything used in or about the mails, telegraphs, or telephones, or in the working thereof, or by any other means have obstructed the mail service, or the sending of messages by such telegraphs or telephones, shall be punished with penal servitude for a period of not exceeding three years, or by the imposition of a fine of not exceeding one hundred *yen*.

SECTION VI.

Of the Violation of Domicile, Burglary, and Housebreaking.

Article 163.

Whosoever, without cause (without lawful {excuse / motive} ?) shall have invaded (entered by force) an inhabited or protected house, building, or ship, and not retired (gone away) when requested so to do, shall be punished with penal servitude for a period not exceeding one year or a fine of not exceeding fifty *yen*.

Under the following circumstances the punishment shall be penal servitude for a period not exceeding three years:—

1. If the entry was effected at night:
2. If the entry has been effected by scaling or breaking, gateways or walls, or by breaking, forcing, or opening locks and bolts:
3. If the intruder carried any dangerous or offensive weapon or instrument:
4. If the offender has committed violence or been guilty of intimidation by menace of injury:
5. When the offenders are of the number of two or more.

Article 164.

Persons who have committed the offences mentioned in the preceding article with intent to commit larceny (settō) or robbery (gō-tō) shall be punished with penal servitude for a period not exceeding five years.

Article 165.

Persons who have, without cause (without lawful {excuse / motive} ?) invaded (entered by force) the Imperial palaces or gardens attached thereto, a temporary Imperial sojourning place, or an Imperial sepulchre, shall be punished with penal servitude for a period of not exceeding five years.

ARTICLE 166.

The offences mentioned in this Section are punishable even if not actually consummated.

ARTICLE 167.

Persons who have committed offences mentioned in this section *may* alsc be placed under police surveillance.

SECTION VII.

OF THF BETRAYAL AND REVELATION OF SECRETS.

ARTICLE 168.

Whosoever shall have unlawfully opened personal letters,* and other documents of a private nature, or secreted the same, shall be punished with imprisonment for a period not exceeding six months or a fine of not exceeding fifty *yen*.

ARTICLE 169.

Doctors, midwives, druggists, advocates (barristers), public notaries, and ministers of religion, who, being possessors of secrets entrusted to them or coming to their knowledge by reason of their position or profession, shall have disclosed the same, shall be punished either with penal servitude for a period not exceeding six months, imprisonment for a period not exceeding six months, or a fine of not exceeding two hundred *yen*. However the

*Compare Art. XXVI of the Constitution of Japan.—"*Except in cases mentioned in the law, the secrecy of the letters of every Japanese subject shall remain inviolate.*"

statements (i.e. revelations) which the above, mentioned persons shall have made to government offices shall not be punishable.

Article 170.

The prosecution for offences mentioned in this section shall only take place on the complaint of the injured party.

CHAPTER VII.

Of Offences against Public Health.

SECTION I.

Of the Trade in, and Use of, Opium.

Article 171.

Whosoever shall have imported, manufactured, or sold, opium (intended to be smoked) shall be punished with penal servitude for a period not exceeding five years.

Article 172.

Whosoever shall have imported, manufactured, or sold, instruments or apparatus suitable for the smoking of opium, shall be punished with penal servitude for a period not exceeding three years.

Article 173.

Customs officials who shall have permitted the import of opium, or of instruments or apparatus suitable for the smoking of opium, shall be punished with penal servitude for a period not exceeding seven years.

Article 174.

Whosoever shall have supplied premises to smoke opium in, and shall have made personal profit by it, shall be punished with penal servitude for a period not exceeding three years.

Article 175.

Every individual who shall have smoked opium shall be punished with penal servitude for a period not exceeding three years.

Article 176.

Every person who shall be found possessor or depositary of opium intended to be smoked, or of instruments suitable for its smoking, shall be punished with penal servitude for a period not exceeding one year.

Article 177.

Persons who have committed any of the offences mentioned in this section, and who are consequently punishable with penal servitude for a period of upwards of one year, shall be placed under police surveillance.

Article 178.

The rules relative to the "*Repetition of Offences*" are also applicable to the case of persons who have committed any of the offences mentioned in this section.

SECTION II.

Of Offences relative to Drinkingwater and to Food-stuffs.

Article 179.

Whosoever shall have polluted drinkable waters, in a manner to render the use of them impossible, shall be punished with penal servitude for a period not exceeding three months or a fine of not exceeding fifty *yen*.

ARTICLE 180.

Whosoever shall have polluted drinkable water supplied to the public by means of water-works, or polluted the source of such water supply in a manner to render its use impossible, shall be punished with penal servitude for a period not exceeding five years.

ARTICLE 181.

Whosoever shall have poisoned drinkable waters, or polluted them with other substances injurious to health, shall be punished with penal servitude for a period not exceeding three years.

ARTICLE 182.

Whosoever shall have poisoned or polluted drinkable waters supplied to the public by means of water-works, or poisoned or polluted the source of such waters with substances injurious to health, shall be punished with limited penal servitude: if death has resulted from the aforesaid poisoning or pollution, the offender shall be punished with either death, perpetual penal servitude, or penal servitude for a period of not less than seven years.

ARTICLE 183.

Whosoever shall have damaged or obstructed water-mains, pipes, or aqueducts, by means of which supplies of drinking-water are furnished to the public, shall be punished with penal servitude for a period not exceeding ten years: if inundation or flooding has been caused, comparison shall be made with the provisions of the law relating to inundations, and the offender shall be sentenced to the most severe penalty provided.

Article 184.

Whosoever shall have placed on sale drinks or foods destined for human consumption and containing additions $\frac{\text{and}}{\text{or}}$ mixtures injurious to health, shall be punished with penal servitude for a period not exceeding three months or a fine not exceeding fifty *yen*.

Article 185.

In the cases foreseen in Articles 179, 180, 181, and 184, if the death or illness of any person has been occasioned, the penalties for "Wounding and (grievous) bodily harm" shall be applied, according as they are more severe than the preceding.

SECTION III.

Of Offences against the Sanitary Regulations.

Article 186.

Whosoever shall have infringed the general regulations established for the purpose of preventing the spread of contagious (epidemic) diseases, and landed from any ship of war or other vessel, held communication with the shore, or any other ship of war or other vessel, or landed objects (disembarked goods?), shall be punished with imprisonment not exceeding one year, or a fine not exceeding two hundred *yen*.

A commander of a war-ship, or a captain of any other vessel, or whosoever shall be acting in such capacity who has himself committed any of the offences mentioned in the preceding paragraph, caused such offences to be committed, or knowingly permitted them to be committed, shall be punished with imprisonment for a period not exceeding two years or a fine of not exceeding five hundred *yen*.

Article 187.

A commander of a war-ship or a captain of any other vessel, or a person performing the functions of commander or captain, who has infringed the general regulations established for the purpose of preventing the spread of contagious (epidemic) diseases, and caused such vessel to proceed on a voyage or to come to anchor, shall be punished with imprisonment for a period not exceeding three years, or a fine of not exceeding one thousand *yen*.

Article 188.

Whosoever shall have in any way other than mentioned in the two foregoing articles infringed the general regulations established for the purpose of preventing the spread of contagious diseases, shall be punished with imprisonment for a period not exceeding six months, or a fine of not exceeding one hundred *yen*.

Article 189.

Whosoever shall have infringed the general regulations established for the purpose of preventing the spread of murrain among animals, shall be punished with imprisonment for a period not exceeding three months or a fine of not exceeding fifty *yen*.

Article 190.

When a doctor who has been ordered to make a medical examination of a person suffering from a contagious disease, or to examine the virus of such disease, refuses without due cause to comply with the order, he shall be punished with a fine of not exceeding fifty *yen*.

The same applies to a doctor who has been ordered to examine cattle suffering from a contagious disease, or to examine the virus of such disease, and who has refused to make the examination without due cause.

SECTION IV.

Of the illegal Practice of Medicine.

Article 191.

Every person who shall have practised the profession of medicine (i.e. as a physician or surgeon) without having obtained full license to do so, shall be punished with a fine of not exceeding one hundred *yen*.

Article 192.

Every person who shall have practised as a veterinary surgeon without having obtained full license to do so, shall be punished with a fine of not exceeding fifty *yen*.

CHAPTER VIII.

Of Offences against Public Trust.

SECTION I.

Counterfeit Money.

Article 193.

Whosoever shall have counterfeited or altered* current coins or paper money of the realm, with intent to utter the same, shall be punished with penal servitude for life or for a period of upward of three years.

Article 194.

He who shall have counterfeited or altered foreign gold and silver coins having circulation in Japan, with intent to utter the same, shall be punished with limited penal servitude for a period of upwards of one year.

*The word "alter" (*henzō*) also implies "colouring, altering impairing, diminishing, lightening, clipping, and defacing."

Article 195.

He who shall have imported into Japan counterfeited or altered coins or notes, or counterfeited or altered foreign gold and silver coins, shall be punished as if he had been guilty of counterfeiting and altering.

Article 196.

Whosoever shall have received, with intent to utter, counterfeited or altered monies or notes, or, foreign gold and silver coins, shall be punished with penal servitude for a period of not exceeding three years, and he who has actually uttered and put off the same shall be punished with penal servitude for a period not exceeding ten years.

Article 197.

The attempt to commit the offences mentioned in the four foregoing articles is punishable under the heading of "infractions not consummated."

Article 198.

Whosoever shall have received Japanese counterfeit or altered coins or notes, or counterfeit foreign gold and silver coins, and knowingly uttered the same after obtaining knowledge of the fact that they were counterfeit or altered, shall be fined in a sum of not exceeding treble the value of the monies so uttered; but the fine shall in no case be less than one *yen*.

Article 199.

Persons who shall have knowingly prepared and provided tools, instruments, or materials, for the purpose of counterfeiting or altering monies and notes as mentioned in Articles 193 and 194, shall be punished with penal servitude for a period not exceeding five years.

ARTICLE 200.

Persons who have committed the offences mentioned in this section, and who are punishable with perpetual penal servitude, shall be sentenced to deprivation of civic rights, and those punishable with penal servitude for a period of upwards of one year shall be deprived of civic rights and placed under police surveillance. Persons punishable with less than one year's penal servitude *may* be deprived of their civic rights, and placed under police surveillance.

SECTION II.

OF THE FORGERY OF INSTRUMENTS.

ARTICLE 201.

Whosoever shall have, with intent to utter same, fraudulently used a counterfeit of the Imperial Privy Seal, a counterfeit of the Great Seal of the Empire, or a counterfeit of the Imperial Sign Manual, or shall have improperly used the Privy Seal, Great Seal, or Sign Manual and forged Imperial or other documents, shall be punished either with perpetual penal servitude or with penal servitude for a period of not less than seven years.

Whosoever shall have, with intent to utter same, fraudulently altered* a document to which is attached the Imperial Privy Seal, the Great Seal of the Empire, or the Imperial Sign Manual, shall be punished in the same manner (as provided in the foregoing paragraph).

ARTICLE 202.

Whosoever shall have, with intent to utter same, fraudulently used a counterfeit of an official or public

---

**Zō-gen hen-kan*:—to add to, to decrease, to alter and to change.

seal, or shall have improperly used official or public seals, stamps, marks or signatures and forged official or public instruments, shall be punished with penal servitude for a period not exceeding ten years.

The same penalty shall be imposed upon whosoever shall have, with intent to utter same, fraudulently altered an official or public document to which is attached an official or public seal or the seal or signature of a government or public official.

Apart from the (cases contemplated in the) two foregoing paragraphs, whosoever shall have, with intent to utter same, fraudulently forged or altered official or public documents which should be drawn up by government or public officials, shall be punished either with penal servitude for a period not exceeding one year or a fine of not exceeding fifty *yen*.

Article 203.

Every person who shall have, with intent to utter the same, fabricated fraudulent documents relative to the functions of government or public officials, or fraudulently altered such documents, shall be punished in accordance with the provisions of the two preceding articles, cognizance being taken as to whether the seals and signatures exist or otherwise.

Article 204.

Whosoever shall have, with intent to utter the same, used a counterfeid seal or a forged signature or improperly used the (genuine) seal or signature of another and fabricated documents relative to rights and obligations-shall be punished with penal servitude for a period not exceeding five years.

The same penalty shall be imposed upon whosoever shall have, with intent to utter the same, fraudulently altered (falsified) a document relative to rights and obligations to which is attached the (genuine) seal or signature of another person.

ARTICLE 205.

Whosoever shall have, by means of practising deceit upon Government or Public officials, caused false entries to be made in census registers, registration books, or in any notarially recorded deeds relating to rights and obligations, shall be punished with penal servitud, for a period not exceeding two years, or with a fine of not exceeding one hundred *yen*.

Attempts to commit the offences mentioned in this article are punishable under the heading of "*infractions not consummated.*"

ARTICLE 206.

Whosoever shall have made fraudulent statements in medical certificates or certificates of death handed in to doctors, Government offices, or Public offices, shall be punished with penal servitude for a period not exceeding three years, or with a fine of not exceeding one hundred *yen*.

ARTICLE 207.

Whosoever shall have uttered documents mentioned in Articles 201 and 206 shall be punished in the same manner as he who has forged or fraudulently altered them, or caused them to be so forged, altered, and falsified. Attempts to commit the offences mentioned in this Article are punishable under the heading of "*infractions not consummated.*"

ARTICLE 208.

Persons who have committed offences mentioned in this section, and who in consequence are punishable with perpetual penal servitude, may be deprived of their civic rights; while persons who are punishable with limited penal servitude may be sentenced to deprivation of civic rights and be placed under police surveillance.

SECTION III.

Of the Forgery of valuable Securities.

Article 209.

Whosoever shall have, with intent to utter the same, forged, falsified, or fraudulently endorsed Government bonds, Share certificates of Companies, Bills, Notes, Cheques, or other instruments saleable (negotiable ?) on endorsement; or any convertible paper, shall be punished with penal servitude for a period not exceeding ten years.

The penalty is the same for uttering any of the above instruments.

Attempts to commit the offences mentioned in this Article are punishable under the heading of "*infractions not consummated.*"

Article 210.

Persons who have committed offences mentioned in the preceding article, and who are in consequence punishable with penal servitude for a term of one year and upwards shall be sentenced to deprivation of civic rights and to police surveillance.

SECTION IV.

Of the Forgery of Seals.

Article 211.

Whosoever shall have, with intent to use the same, fraudulently counterfeited the Imperial Privy Seal, the

Great Seal of the Empire, or the Imperial Sign Manual shall be punished with perpetual penal servitude.

Whosoever shall have improperly used the Imperial Privy Seal, the Great Seal of the Empire, or, the Imperial Sign Manual, shall be punished in the same manner (as provided in the foregoing paragraph).

ARTICLE 212.

Whosoever shall have, with intent to use the same, fraudulently counterfeited a Government or Public seal, or the seals or signatures of Government or Public officials, shall be punished with penal servitude for a period not exceeding five years.

The same penalty shall be imposed upon whosoever shall.have made improper use of a Government or Public Seal, or the seals or signatures of Government or Public officials.

ARTICLE 213.

Whosoever shall have, with intent to use the same fraudulently counterfeited the official mark of a Government or Public office, shall be punished with penal servitude for a period not exceeding three years.

The same penalty shall be imposed upon whosoever shall have made improper use of the official mark of a Government or Public office.

ARTICLE 214.

Whosoever shall have, with intent to use the same fraudulently counterfeited the seal or signature of another person shall be punished with penal servitude for a period not exceeding three years.

The same penalty shall be imposed upon whosoever shall.have made improper use of the seal or signature of another person.

Article 215.

Whosoever shall have, with intent to utter the same, fraudulently counterfeited any kind of stamps, (stamped) note and bill forms, postage stamps, (stamped) envelopes, postcards, and wrappers issued by Government, or any postage stamps, (stamped) envelopes, post-cards, or wrappers issued by the Government of any country belonging to the Postal Union, shall be punished with penal servitude for a period not exceeding five years.

The same penalty shall be imposed upon whosoever shall have uttered the stamps, (stamped) note and bill forms, postage stamps, (stamped) envelopes, post-cards, or wrappers mentioned in the foregoing paragraph.

Article 216.

Attempts to commit the offences mentioned in this Section are punishable under the heading of "infractions not consummated."

Article 217.

Persons who have committed offences mentioned in this section, and who in consequence are punishable with penal servitude for a period of one year and upwards, *may* be sentenced to deprivation of civic rights and police surveillance.

SECTION V.

Of false Weights and Measures.

Article 218.

Whosoever shall have manufactured weights or measures which are at variance with the official standards, or placed them on sale, shall be punished with penal servitude for a period not exceeding three years.

Whosoever shall, with the intent to use them in his business, be in the possession of false weights or measures (*i.e.* weights and measures at variance with the prescribed standards) shall be punished with penal servitude for a period not exceeding one year, or a fine of not exceeding two hundred *yen*.

Article 219.

Whosoever shall manufacture, repair, or place on sale, weights or measures, without being duly licensed, shall be fined in a sum not exceeding three hundred *yen*.

The same provision applies to whosoever shall sell weights and measures which have not been duly inspected and approved.

Whosoever shall, with the intent to use them in his business, be in the possession of weights and measures which have not been (officially) inspected and approved, shall be fined in a sum not exceeding one hundred *yen*.

SECTION VI.

Of Perjury.

Article 220.

Whosoever shall have made a false statement after having been sworn in as a witness in a Court of Judicial Administration, a Court of Administrative Litigation, or any other Court of Justice, shall be punished with penal servitude for a period of not exceeding ten years.

If the penalty of death has been undergone by the victim of the perjury the punishment shall be penal servitude for life, or for a period of not less than five years.

ARTICLE 221.

The punishments provided in the foregoing Article *may* be remitted either in whole or in part, if the offender shall have retracted his false declarations prior to final and conclusive judgment being rendered in the case which his evidence affects.

ARTICLE 222.

The provisions of the two preceding Articles apply to experts and interpreters who shall have (knowingly) given false evidence, or made a false interpretation while under oath.

ARTICLE 223.

Persons who have committed offences mentioned in this section, and who in consequence are punishable with perpetual penal servitude or with penal servitude for a period of one year and upwards, *may* be sentenced to deprivation of civic rights.

SECTION VII.

OF FALSE ACCUSATION.

ARTICLE 224.

Whosoever shall have made a complaint or statement* which he knows to be false, with the intention of procuring the criminal or disciplinary punishment of an innocent person, shall be punished in accordance with the provisions of Articles 220 and 223.

ARTICLE 225.

Although a person may have made a false accusation, if he voluntary denounces himself and retracts before the judgment becomes irrevocable, the punishment *may* be remitted either in whole or in part.

* *Koku-so*=a complaint or accusation, *Koku-hatsu*=criminal information, *Shin-koku*=a statement made to officials.

The same applies to the case of a person who voluntarily denounces himself and retracts previous to the infliction of a disciplinary punishment imposable (upon a third party) in an Administrative Government Office.

CHAPTER IX.

Of Offences against Public Morals.

SECTION I.

On Indecency, Adultery, and Bigamy.

Article 226.

Whosoever shall have publicly committed an indecent act shall be punished by the imposition of a fine.

Article 227.

Whosoever shall have publicly exhibited or sold indecent (obscene) pictures or other objects shall be punished as provided in the preceding Article.

The rules relative to the levying and collecting of fines are applicable to persons who have committed offences mentioned in this Article.

Article 228.

Whosoever shall have committed an indecent act against a child of either sex of less than twelve years of age shall be punished with penal servitude for a period of not exceeding five years.

Whosoever shall have committed an indecent act with violence and threats against a person of either sex whose age exceeds twelve years shall be punished with penal servitude for a period of not exceeding three years.

Article 229.

Whosoever shall have obtained carnal knowledge of a woman or a girl by means of violence and threats shall be adjudged guilty of rape and punished with penal servitude for a period not exceeding ten years.

Unlawful intercourse with a female child of less than twelve years of age shall be punished in the same manner.

Whosoever shall have taken advantage of mental derangement, loss of reason, or of incapacity to make resistance, and obtained carnal knowledge of a woman or girl, shall be considered as guilty of rape.

Article 230.

Attempts to commit the offences mentioned in the two preceding Articles are punishable under the heading of "*infractions not consummated.*"

Article 231.

As regards the offences mentioned in Articles 228 and 229 the procecution shall only take place on the complaint of the injured person.

Article 232.

Whosoever shall have occasioned death or wounds owing to the committal of rape shall be punished with penal servitude for life or for upwards of five years.

Article 233.

Whosoever shall have, for purposes of gain, urged and encouraged a hitherto virtuous woman or girl to commit fornication shall be punished with penal servitude for a period not exceeding one year or with a fine of not exceeding one hundred *yen*.

Article 234.

A married woman guilty of adultery, as well as her co-actor in the crime, shall be punished with penal servitude for a period of not exceeding one year.

The prosecution for adultery shall only take place on the complaint of the husband, but the complaint shall be of no effect if he has previously encouraged the aforesaid adultery.

Article 235.

Whosover, being lawfully married, shall have contracted another legal marriage shall be punished with penal servitude for a period of not exceeding two years.

Article 236.

Persons who have committed offences mentioned in Articles 228, 229, and 232, and who in consequence are punishable with perpetual penal servitude, or with penal servitude for a period of one year and upwards, *shall* be sentenced to deprivation of civic rights.

SECTION II.

Of Gambling, Lotteries, and Games of Chance.

Article 237.

Whosoever shall have played, bet, or wagered, a valuable thing (*zai-motsu*) as a stake, with regard to a matter depending upon chance or contingency, shall be punished with a fine of not exceeding one hundred *yen*. This provision does not however apply to a case where an article (*buppin*) is merely wagered for the sake of momentary amusement or pleasure.

Article 238.

Whosoever shall have made a regular practice of wagering or gaming shall be punished with penal servitude for a period not exceeding three years.

Whosoever shall have, for the sake of profit, opened a gaming house, or shall have formed an association of gamblers for the same purpose, shall be punished with penal servitude for a period not exceeding five years.

The provisions of the Code relative to the "Repeti, tion of Offences" are applicable to persons guilty of the offences mentioned in this Article.

Article 239.

Whosoever shall have, *without being duly authorised,* sold lottery tickets, shall be punished with penal servitude for a period of not exceeding one year, or with a fine of not exceeding one thousand *yen.*

Whosoever shall have acted as a medium or agent in selling lottery tickets shall be punished with penal servitude for a period of not exceeding six months, or with a fine of not exceeding two hundred *yen.*

The provisions of this Code relative to the "Repetition of Offences" are applicable to persons guilty of the offences mentioned in this Article.

Article 240.

Whosoever shall have, without being duly authorized, purchased lottery tickets, shall be punished with a fine of not exceeding twenty *yen.*

Article 241.

Persons who have committed any of the offences mentioned in this section, and who are consequently punishable swith penal servitude for a period of upwards of one year shall be placed under police surveillance.

SECTION III.

Of Offenses relating to Shrines and Temples and to the Bodies of the Dead.

Article 242.

Every person who shall have committed an insulting act against a shrine, temple, cemetery, or any place of religious worship, shall be punished with penal servitude for a period not exceeding six months, or with a fine of not exceeding fifty *yen*.

The penalty shall be penal servitude for a period not exceeding one year, or a fine of not exceeding one hundred *yen* if the offender has disturbed or interfered with the preaching or other religious exercises (*sekkyō, mata wa reihai wo bō-gai shitaru*).

Article 243.

Whosoever shall have mutilated or abandoned the body or remains of a deceased person shall be punished with penal servitude for a period not exceeding one year.

Article 244.

Whosoever shall have been found guilty of violation of interment, or of damaging a tomb, shall be punished with penal servitude for a period not exceeding two years.

If therefore the offender has exposed in the open air, abandoned, or mutilated, the body or remains of a deceased person, the penalty shall be penal servitude for a period not exceeding three years.

Article 245.

Attempts to commit any of the offenses mentioned in the foregoing three Articles shall be punished even if the offenses are not actually consummated.

Article 246.

Whosoever shall have exhumed and reinterred a corpse without having received due permission so to do shall be punished with a fine.

CHAPTER X.

Of Crimes and Delicts committed by Public Servants in the Exercise of their Functions.

Article 247.

Every government or public official who, acting in this capacity, shall have abused his power and shall have caused a person to commit an act which he had no right to commit, or shall have unduly hindered him from exercising a legal capacity, shall be punished with imprisonment for a period not exceeding six months.

Article 248.

Every magistrate, prosecuting official, or officer of police (or person acting in such capacity, or person acting as assistant to such officials) who acting in his official capacity shall have abused his power and (illegally) arrested, taken into custody, or detained, an individual shall be punished with penal servitude or with imprisonment for a period not exceeding five years.

Article 249.

Every magistrate, prosecuting official, or officer of police (or person acting in such capacity or person acting as assistant to such officials), or every person acting as gaoler or guard over prisoners, who shall have used towards a prisoner violence or bad treatment shall be punished with penal servitude, or with imprisonment for a period not exceeding five years.

ARTICLE 250.

If, on account of the offenses mentioned in the two preceding Articles, there has resulted death or wounds, the penalties for "*Wounding and (grievous) bodily harm*" shall be compared with (those provided above) and the more severe penalty shall be inflicted.

ARTICLE 251.

Every gaoler or guard who, in case of inundation, conflagration, hurricane, earthquake, or other extraordinary event (of a calamitous nature) shall have failed to take, or cause to be taken, the necessary steps to avoid disaster, and thus have caused death or wounds to the prisoners, shall be punished according to the provisions *re* "*Wounding and (grievous) bodily harm.*"

ARTICLE 252.

Every government official, public official, member of a conference or deliberative assembly, or arbitrator, who shall have received bribes, or any other kind of valuable gift, advantage, or emolument, or who shall have entered into an agreement to receive the same in connection with his official capacity and duties, shall be punished with penal servitude for a period not exceeding three years and a fine of not exceeding three hundred *yen*.

Persons who have committed dishonestly improper acts, or who have not acted properly and befittingly, shall be punished with penal servitude for a period not exceeding five years and a fine of not exceeding five hundred *yen*: should the offender be a magistrate or arbitrator the penalty shall be penal servitude for a period not exceeding ten years and a fine of not exceeding one thousand *yen*.

Under the circumstances foreseen in the two preceding paragraphs, should the amount of bribe, or any other kind of valuable gift, advantage, or emolument received be greater than that of the maximum fine provided, a fine may then be imposed not exceeding the amount or value of the bribe taken by the accused.

ARTICLE 253.

Whosoever shall have given, offered, or agreed to give, a bribe or any other valuable gift, advantage or emolument to any government official, member of a conference or deliberative assembly, or arbitrator, shall be punished with penal servitude for a period not exceeding three years, and a fine of not exceeding three hundred *yen*.

ARTICLE 254.

Although he may not have received bribes, valuable gifts, advantages, or emoluments, yet the government official, public official, member of a conference or deliberative assembly, or arbitrator, who has been guilty of a dishonestly improper act, or of not acting properly and befittingly, owing to favoritism or hatred, shall be punished in accordance with the provisions of Article 252, paragraph 2.

ARTICLE 255.

Every government official, public official, member of a conference or deliberative assembly, or arbitrator, who for his own advantage, or for the sake of conferring an advantage on some other person, shall have divulged the secrets of his office, shall be punished with penal servitude for a period not exceeding three years and a fine of not exceeding three hundred *yen*.

ARTICLE 256.

Persons who have committed any of the offenses mentioned in Articles 252 to 255, and who are in consequence punishable with upwards of one year's penal servitude, *shall* be sentenced to deprivation of civic rights.

CHAPTER XI.

OF OFFENSES AGAINST THE LIVES AND PERSONS OF INDIVIDUALS.

SECTION I.

HOMICIDE.

ARTICLE 257.

Whosoever shall have killed another shall be punished with perpetual penal servitude, or with penal servitude for a period of not less than seven years.

ARTICLE 258.

When a person has committed the offense mentioned in the preceding article, and any of the following circumstances exist, he shall be punished either with death or with perpetual penal servitude :—

1. When the offense has been committed against a direct ancestor :
2. When the offense has been committed with premeditation (express malice) :
3. When two or more persons have been killed ;
4. When the offense has been committed by means of mutilation and dismemberment or other acts of barbarity :
5. When the offense has been committed for the purpose of helping the perpetrator in committing

another grave offense, or to assist him in escaping the punishment for an offense already committed;

ARTICLE 259.

Attempts to commit the offenses mentioned in the two preceding articles shall be punished as "*Infractions not consummated.*"

ARTICLE 260.

Persons who have conspired to commit, or made preparations to commit, murder, *may* be placed under police surveillance.

ARTICLE 261.

He who shall have instigated and caused a person to commit suicide, or shall have killed him at his solicitation, shall be punished with penal servitude, or imprisonment, for a period of not less than seven years.

ARTICLE 262.

Persons who have committed any of the offenses mentioned in this Section, and who are punishable with death or perpetual penal servitude, *may* be deprived of their civic rights; those who are punishable with upwards of one year's penal servitude *may* be deprived of their civic rights and placed under police surveillance.

SECTION II.

WOUNDING AND (GRIEVOUS) BODILY HARM.

ARTICLE 263.

Whosoever shall have wounded $\frac{\text{and}}{\text{or}}$ injured or inflicted any (grievous) bodily harm upon any other person, shall be punished with either penal servitude or imprisonment for a period not exceeding five years, or a fine of not exceeding one hundred *yen*.

The same punishments shall be inflicted upon persons who have cut off or damaged the hair of a woman's head.

ARTICLE 264.

When the following effects have resulted from bodily harm inflicted, the punishment shall be penal servitude for a period not exceeding ten years :—

1. Loss of the sight of one eye or both eyes :
2. Loss of the hearing of one ear or both ears :
3. Loss of speech :
4. Loss of the use of one or more limbs :
5. Loss of the use of the sexual organs :
6. Serious and incurable mental or bodily disease :
7. Miscarriage.

ARTICLE 265.

Whosoever shall have caused the death of a person by means of wounding or inflicting any grievous bodily harm, shall be punished with limited penal servitude.

When the offense has been committed against direct ancestors the punishment shall be penal servitude for life or for upwards of seven years.

ARTICLE 266.

In the event of any of the offenses mentioned in the three preceding Articles being committed, any person present who shall have aided or abetted the perpetrator (even although he personally may not have been guilty of inflicting injuries) shall be punished with penal servitude for a period of not exceeding one year, or a fine of not exceeding fifty *yen*.

If the violence has been committed by two or more persons, and it is not possible to find out the nature or gravity of the violence committed by each of the offenders, they shall be dealt with according to the provisions relating to the "*co-operation of several persons in the same offense**" even although no conspiracy existed between them.

ARTICLE 267.

Persons who have been guilty of assault ("*violent conduct*") without going to the length of actual wounding or inflicting bodily harm, shall be punished with detention or police fine.

The prosecution for the offense mentioned in this Article shall only take place on the complaint of the injured party.

SECTION III.

OF INVOLUNTARY HOMICIDE, BLOWS, OR WOUNDS.

ARTICLE 268.

Whosoever, by negligence, shall have caused wounding or bodily harm, shall be punished with a fine of not exceeding one hundred *yen*.

The prosecution for the offense mentioned in this Article shall only take place on the complaint of the injured party.

ARTICLE 269.

Whosoever, by negligence, shall have (involuntarily) committed homicide shall be punished with a fine of not exceeding two hundred *yen*.

ARTICLE 270.

Whosoever, by reason of a dereliction of duty and failure to take necessary precautions in connection with

* *Vide* Chapt. VII. Articles 77—83.

his specific functions, shall have (involuntarily) committed homicide or caused wounds and bodily injury, shall be punished with imprisonment for a period not exceeding three years, or with a fine of not exceeding five hundred *yen*.

SECTION IV.

Of Abortion.

Article 271.

Whosoever shall have procured abortion for a woman shall be punished with penal servitude for a period not exceeding five years.

Attempts to commit the offense mentioned in this Article are punishable under the heading of "*infractions not consummated.*"

Article 272.

When a person has committed the offense mentioned in the preceding Article, and thereby caused death or injury to a woman, the provisions (of the Chapter relating to) *wounding and grievous bodily harm* shall be compared with (those of the above Article) and the case decided according to the most severe of the two laws.

Article 273.

Whosoever shall have procured abortion for a woman, either at her request or with her consent, shall be punished with penal servitude for a period not exceeding six months; and whosoever shall have thereby caused death or injury to the woman shall be punished with penal servitude for a period not exceeding three years.

Article 274.

Any doctor, midwife, or chemist, who shall have procured abortion for a woman either at her request or with her consent shall be punished with penal servitude for a period of not exceeding three years; and whosoever shall have thereby caused death or injury to the woman shall be punished with penal servitude for a period not exceeding five years.

The same penalty shall be pronounced against those who shall have procured abortion for a woman at her request in consideration of pecuniary reward.

Article 275.

Every woman enceinte who shall have (willingly) procured abortion by the administration of drugs, or by the aid of any other means, shall be punished with penal servitude for a period not exceeding five years.

SECTION V.

Of Abandoning Children, the Aged, Sick, or Infirm.

Article 276.

Whosoever shall have abandoned or deserted a child, or a person who requires assistance owing to sickness, shall be punished with penal servitude for a period not exceeding three years.

Article 277.

Whosoever, being charged with the responsibility of protecting an old person, a child, or a sick person, abandons, or deserts his charges, or fails to afford them protection necessary to the preservation of their lives, shall be punished with penal servitude for a period of not exceeding five years.

Persons who have been guilty of the offenses mentioned in the preceding paragraph *vis-à-vis* direct ancestors or elder relations within the first degree of consanguinity, shall be punished with penal servitude for a period not exceeding seven years.

Article 278.

Persons who have been guilty of the offenses mentioned in the two preceding Articles, and thereby caused death or bodily injury to individuals, shall be punished by comparing the provisions of this chapter with those applicable to *wounding and grievous bodily harm* and inflicting the most severe of the possible penalties.

Article 279.

Whosoever shall have discovered an old person, young child, or sick person, who is in need of succour, and without reasonable cause shall not have rescued him or reported the matter to the public authorities, shall be punished with detention or police fine.

CHAPTER XII.

Of Offenses against the Liberty of the Subject.

SECTION I.

Of Illegal Arrest and False Imprisonment.

Article 280.

Every individual who shall have arbitrarily and illegally arrested or imprisoned a person shall be punished with penal servitude for a period of not exceeding three years.

If the arrest or imprisonment has been accompanied with blows or physical torture, or deprivation of nourishment, or clothing, the penalty shall be penal servitude for a period not exceeding five years.

ARTICLE 281.

If by reason of the committal of the offenses mentioned in the preceding Article death or injury shall have been occasioned, the penalties for *wounding and grievous bodily harm* shall be compared with those provided herein and the case decided in accordance with the most severe of the provisions.

SECTION II.

OF THREATS.

ARTICLE 282.

Whosoever shall be found guilty of having used threats to do injury to life, limb, liberty, reputation, or property, shall be punished with penal servitude for a period not exceeding one year, or a fine of not exceeding one hundred *yen*.

Threats are also punishable in like manner when injury is threatened to the life, person, liberty, reputation, or property of relations, or those allied to the person who has been threatened.

ARTICLE 283.

Whosoever shall have made threats of injury to the life, person, liberty, reputation, or property of an individual, and by means of such threats, accompanied with violent conduct and unlawful compulsion, shall have caused a person to do an act which he had no obligation to do, or hindered him from doing an act which he had a lawful right to perform, shall be punished with penal servitude for a period not exceeding three years.

The same applies to threats against the life, person, liberty, reputation, or property of a person's relations, or those allied to him, by means of which he is caused to do an act which he is under no obligation to do, or hindered from doing an act which he has a lawful right to perform.

Attempts to commit the offenses mentioned in this Article are punishable under the heading of "*infractions not consummated.*"

Article 284.

In all cases where offenses mentioned in this Section have been committed, the trial shall only take place on the complaint of the injured party.

SECTION III.

Of Abduction, Kidnapping, and Alluring.

Article 285.

Whosoever shall have allured or taken away any minor of less than twenty years of age without the sanction of his or her father or mother, or other person having the lawful care or charge of such minor, shall be punished with penal servitude for a period of not exceeding five years.

The same penalty shall be inflicted when the minor, with the consent of his or her father, mother, or curator, has been kidnapped by force or fraudulent stratagem.

Article 286

Whoscever shall have, for the purpose of profiting thereby, kidnapped a person by means of force or fraudulent stratagem, shall be punished with penal servitude for a period of not exceeding ten years.

The same penalty shall be inflicted when the person has been kidnapped by means of force or fraudulent stratagem for immoral purposes, or with the intent to marry.

The prosecution of offenses mentioned in paragraph II shall only take place on the complaint of the injured party or the relations or kindred of such injured party, but if the person kidnapped has actually contracted a marriage he or she cannot lodge a valid complaint until after the marriage has been declared incomplete or invalid by the irrevocable judgment of a Court of Law.

Article 287.

Whosoever shall have, for the purpose of profiting thereby, received a person who has been kidnapped, shall be punished with penal servitude for a period not exceeding seven years.

Article 288.

Whosoever shall have kidnapped a person with the intent to transport him or her out of the Empire, or with the intent to sell such person, shall be punished with limited penal servitude for a term of not less than five years.

The same penalty shall be inflicted upon whosoever shall convey out of the Empire a person who has been sold or kidnapped.

Article 289.

Attempts to commit the offenses mentioned in this Section are punishable under the heading of "*infractions not consummated.*"

CHAPTER XIII.

Of Libel and Indictable Slander.

Article 290.

Whosoever shall have injured the reputation of a person by publicly imputing to him evil acts or disgraceful conduct, shall, irrespective of the fact as to whether the statement relative to the deed or vice imputed to the person is true or false, be punished with penal servitude for a period not exceeding six months, imprisonment, or a fine of not exceeding one hundred *yen*.*

A person who has injured the reputation of the dead is not punishable, except when such injury has arisen in consequence of a false accusation (made before the judicial authorities).

Article 291.

Whosoever shall have publicly insulted and reviled a person shall be punished with detention or police fine, even although he may not have (actually) imputed dishonourable acts or disgraceful conduct to such person.

Article 292.

The prosecution for offenses mentioned in this chapter shall only take place on the complaint of the offended party, or on that of his family or relatives if he is dead.

* The principle underlying this article is that it is no defence to allege that the matter of the libel is true.

CHAPTER IV.

Of Offenses against Property.

SECTION I.

Of Robbery and Theft.

Article 293.

The provisions (of the Chapter) *re the Repetition of Offenses* are applicable to the case of persons who have committed any of the offenses mentioned in this Section.

Article 294.

Attempts to commit the offenses mentioned in this Section are punishable under the heading of "*infractions not consummated.*"

Article 295.

Persons who have committed offenses mentioned in this Section, and who are in consequence punishahle by death or perpetual penal servitude, *shall* be sentenced to deprivation of civic rights; and those persons who are punishable by limited penal servitude for a period of upwards of six months, *shall* be sentenced to deprivation of civic rights and police surveillance. Persons punishable by penal servitude for a period of less than six months *may be* deprived of their civic rights and placed under police surveillance.

Article 296.

Offenses mentioned in this Section shall be free from punishment when they shall have been committed among relations in a *direct* line, or among relations living together, and in the case of other relations no action shall be taken unless a complaint is lodged by the injured party; but the benefit of the present excuse shall not be extended to the co-actors and accomplices (who have not the same standing?).

In the case of robbery with violence the provisions of the preceding paragraph are not applicable.

Article 297.

Even though the property may be that of the offender himself, if such property be hypothecated, or under lien to third persons in a manner investing them with possessionary rights, or if it be under the guard of another person in consequence of orders issued by the authorities, it shall be considered as the property of another person.

SUB-SECTION I.

Larceny.

Article 298.

Whosoever shall have stolen the personal effects of another shall be adjudged guilty of larceny (*sesshu no tsumi*) and punished with penal servitude for a period not exceeding ten years.

SUB-SECTION II.

Article 299.

Whosoever shall have forcibly taken away the personal property of an individual by means of acts of violence or by the aid of threats of injury to the life, person, liberty, or property of another, or to the life, person, liberty or property of a third party whom the person threatened is bound to assist and protect, shall be adjudged guilty of robbery (*gōtō no tsumi*) and punished with limited penal servitude for a period of not less than three years.

Article 300.

Persons who have unlawfully acquired pecuniary advantages by the means mentioned in the preceding article, or have caused third parties to do so, shall be adjudged guilty of robbery.

Article 301.

Should the robber have wounded any person he shall be punished with perpetual penal servitude, or with penal servitude for a period of not less than five years; and if there has been homicide the penalty shall be death or perpetual penal servitude.

Article 302.

If the rape of a woman has been committed on the occasion of a robbery, the penalty shall be perpetual penal servitude, or penal servitude for not less than seven years.

Article 303.

The penalty for robbery shall be pronounced, if, after a person has committed larceny, threats or violence have been resorted to in order to preserve the objects stolen, or for the purpose of escaping punishment.

Article 304.

Whosoever shall have committed larceny by the aid of a suspension of will caused by the use of a narcotic, or by any other means, with the object of committing the theft, shall be considered as guilty of robbery.

Article 305.

Whosoever shall have made preparations or laid plans to commit a robbery shall be placed under police surveillance.

SUB-SECTION III.

Robbery by Intimidation.

Article 306.

Whosoever shall have, by means of intimidation other than those mentioned in Article 299, forcibly taken away the personal property of an individual, shall be adjudged guilty of "*Robbery by Intimidation*" (*Kyō-katsu-tō*) and punished with penal servitude for a period not exceeding ten years.

Article 307.

Whosoever shall have unlawfully acquired pecuniary advantages by the means mentioned in the preceding Article, or have caused third parties to do so, shall be adjudged guilty of "*Robbery by Intimidation.*"

SUB-SECTION IV.

Robbery by Fraud.

Article 308.

Whosoever shall have deceived an individual, and thereby obtained personal property under false pretences, shall be adjudged guilty of "*Robbery by Fraud*" (*Sagi-tō*) and punished with penal servitude for a period not exceeding ten years.

Article 309.

Whosoever shall have unlawfully acquired any pecuniary advantages by the means mentioned in the preceding Article, or have caused third parties to do so, shall be adjudged guilty of "*Robbery by Fraud.*"

Article 310.

Whosoever shall have taken advantage of the weakness or inexperience of a minor and caused to be delivered any property, or shall have unlawfully acquired any pecuniary advantages, or have caused third parties to do so, shall be adjudged guilty of "*Robbery by Fraud.*"

SECTION II.

Embezzlement.

Article 311.

Whosoever shall have unlawfully appropriated either real or personal property which he holds on behalf of another person, shall be punished with penal servitude for a period not exceeding five years.

Even though the personal property may actually appertain to the offender himself, should he take or apply it to his own use after being ordered by the authorities to hold the objects in trust, the same penalty is applicable.

ARTICLE 312.

Whosoever shall have unlawfully taken or applied to his own use either real or personal property which shall have been entrusted to him in the course of his business or professional duties, shall be punished with penal servitude for a period of not exceeding ten years.

Persons who have committed the offenses mentioned in the preceding paragraph, and who are in consequence punishable by upwards of six months penal servitude, *shall* be sentenced to deprivation of civic rights and placed under police surveillance.

ARTICLE 313.

Whosoever shall have obtained possession of lost articles, floating objects (from a shipwreck?), or other articles belonging to another, and shall have appropriated the same, shall be punished in accordance with the provisions of Article 311.

ARTICLE 314.

The provisions of paragraph 1 of Article 296 are applicable to offenses mentioned in this Section.

ARTICLE 315.

The provisions (of the chapter) *re the Repetition of offenses* are applicable to persons who have committed any of the offenses mentioned in this Section.

SECTION III.

Of Receiving Objects Stolen or Embezzled.

Article 316.

Whosoever shall have received objects obtained by means of offenses committed shall be punished with penal servitude for a period of not exceeding five years.

Should the offender be guilty of having lent his assistance to the acts of secretly transmitting or otherwise disposing of stolen goods, or of acting as a depositary of the same, he shall be punished with penal servitude for a period of not exceeding ten years and a fine of not exceeding three hundred *yen.*

The provisions (of the Chapter) *re the Repetition of Offenses* are applicable to persons who have committed any of the offenses mentioned in this Chapter.

Article 317.

Persons who have committed offenses mentioned in the preceding Article, and who are in consequence punishable with penal servitude for a period of upwards of six months, *shall be* sentenced to deprivation of civic rights and to be placed under police surveillance: persons who are punishable with penal servitude for a period of less than six months *may be* deprived of their civic rights and placed under police surveillance.

Article 318.

Offenses mentioned in Article 316 shall be free from punishment when they shall have been committed among relations in a direct line, relations in a direct line by marriage, or among relations living together.

SECTION IV.

Injuries to Property.

Article 319.

Whosoever shall have destroyed documents belonging to the authorities shall be punished with penal servitude for a period of not exceeding seven years.

Whosoever shall have destroyed documents relative to rights and obligations, and belonging to another, shall be punished with penal servitude for a period not exceeding three years, but the prosecution shall only take place on the complaint of the injured person.

Article 320.

Whosoever shall have unlawfully destroyed or injured houses or other buildings belonging to another, shall be punished with penal servitude for a period not exceeding five years.

If there has resulted death or bodily injuries, the penalties for "*Wounding and (grievous) bodily harm*" shall be applied, each time that they are more severe than the preceding.

Article 321.

If any objects other than those mentioned in the two preceding Articles have been destroyed, injured, or wounded, the penalty shall be penal servitude for a period not exceeding two years or a fine of not exceeding one hundred *yen*, but the prosecution shall only take place on the complaint of the injured person.

Article 322.

Even when the property destroyed or injured actually belongs to the offender, if it be under attachment, lien, hypothecation, or mortgage, or if it be insured, the provisions of Articles 319 to 321 are applicable.

IN PREPARATION.

Notes on the Commercial Code of Japan, by F. Schroeder. In these notes which now appear in the "Eastern World," and will be ready for publication in book form in about August next, especial attention is paid to the German sources of the Japanese Code, and to points on which doubt and differences are likely to arise, so that the book will be a reliable guide both to professional men and practical merchants.

ANNOUNCEMENT.

After the completion of the "Notes on the Commercial Code of Japan" Mr. Schroeder intends to write similar commentaries also to the Criminal Code, to the Code of Criminal Procedure, and to publish a revised and enlarged third edition of his "Notes on the Civil Code of Japan," with reference to such cases as may in the meantime have been decided under those Codes and have become known to him. Yokohama, February 1899.

Printed in Dunstable, United Kingdom

91221354R00058